small group bible studies

1 AND 2 PETER

LETTERS TO PEOPLE IN TROUBLE

STUDIES IN THIS SERIES

Available from Marshall Pickering

How to Start a Small Group Bible Study
A Guide to Discussion Study

Mark (recommended as first unit of study)

Acts

Romans

Four Men of God Abraham, Joseph, Moses, David

Genesis

John Book 1 (chapters 1–10)

John Book 2 (chapters 11–21)

1 Corinthians

1 & 2 Peter

Courage to Cope

Psalms & Proverbs

Ephesians and Philemon

1&2 peter

LETTERS TO PEOPLE IN TROUBLE

10 DISCUSSIONS FOR GROUP BIBLE STUDY
BY MARILYN KUNZ AND CATHERINE SCHELL

MARSHALL PICKERING

William Collins Sons & Co. Ltd
London · Glasgow · Sydney · Auckland
Toronto · Johannesburg

First published in the USA in 1971 by Neighborhood
Bible Studies Inc.

This edition first published in Great Britain in 1990 by
Marshall Pickering

Marshall Pickering is an imprint of
Collins Religious Division,
part of the Collins Publishing Group
8 Grafton Street, London W1X 3LA

Copyright © 1971 Marilyn Kunz and Catherine Schell

Printed and bound in Hong Kong

contents

contents

How to Use
This Discussion Guide

Sharing leadership — why and how

Each study guide in the Small Group Bible Study series is prepared with the intention that the ordinary adult group will, by using this guide, be able to rotate the leadership of the discussion. Those who are outgoing in personality are more likely to volunteer to lead first, but within a few weeks it should be possible for almost everyone to have the privilege of directing a discussion session. Everyone, including people new to the Bible who may not yet have committed themselves to Christ, should take a turn in leading by asking the questions from the study guide.

Reasons for this approach are:

1. The discussion leader will prepare in greater depth than the average participant.

2. The experience of leading a study stimulates a person to be a better participant in the discussions led by others.

3. Members of the group which changes discussion leadership weekly tend to feel that the group belongs to everyone in it. It is not "Mr. or Mrs. Smith's Bible Study."

4. The Christian who by reason of spiritual maturity and wider knowledge of the Bible is equipped to be a spiritual leader in the group is set free to *listen* to everyone in the group in a way that is not possible when leading the discussion. He (she) takes his regular turn in leading as it comes around, but if he leads the first study in a series he must guard against the temptation to bring a great deal of outside knowledge and source material which would make others feel they could not possibly attempt to follow his example of leadership.

For study methods and discussion techniques refer to the first booklet in this series, *How to Start a Small Group Bible Study*, as well as to the following suggestions.

How to prepare to participate in a study using this guide

1/ Read through the designated chapter of 1 or 2 Peter daily during the week. Use it in your daily time of meditation and prayer, asking God to teach you what he has for you in it.

2/ Take two or three of the guide questions each day and try to answer them from the passage. Use these questions as tools to dig deeper into the passage. In this way you can cover all the guide questions before the group discussion.

3/ Use the summary questions to tie together the whole chapter in your thinking.

4/ *As an alternative* to using this study in your daily quiet time, spend at least two hours in sustained study once during the week, using the above suggestions.

If you prepare well for each study session, you will find that these letters have much to challenge, strengthen and mature you in your spiritual life. If you are unwilling to prepare well, 1 and 2 Peter will seem confusing and difficult.

How to prepare to lead a study

1/ Follow the above suggestions on preparing to participate in a study. Pray for wisdom and the Holy Spirit's guidance.

2/ Familiarize yourself with the study guide questions until you can rephrase them in your own words if necessary to make you comfortable using them in the discussion.

3/ Some of the studies will require two sessions. It is *not* recommended that you spend *more than two* sessions on one chapter. Each session should run from an hour to an hour and a half.

4/ Pray for the ability to guide the discussion with love and understanding.

How to lead a study

1/ Begin with prayer for minds open to understand and

hearts willing to obey the Word of the Lord. You may ask another member of the group to pray if you have asked him ahead of time.

2/ Have the Bible portion read aloud by paragraphs. Be sure to have the reading done by paragraph or thought units, *never* verse by verse. It is not necessary for everyone to read aloud, or for each to read an equal amount.

3/ Guide the group to discover what the passage says by asking the discussion questions. Use the suggestions from the section on "How to encourage everyone to participate."

4/ As the group discusses the Bible passage together, encourage each one to be honest in self-appraisal. You must take the lead in spiritual honesty. Try to avoid hypocrisy in any form.

5/ Allow time at the end of the discussion to answer the summary questions which help to tie the whole study together.

6/ Bring the discussion to a close at the end of the time allotted. Ask one of the group members to read the conclusion section. Close in a prayer relevant to what has been discussed.

How to encourage everyone to participate

1/ Encourage discussion by asking several people to contribute answers to a question. "What do the rest of you think?" or "Is there anything else which could be added?" are ways of encouraging discussion.

2/ Be flexible and skip any questions which do not fit into the discussion as it progresses.

3/ Deal with irrelevant issues by suggesting that the purpose of your study is to discover what is *in the passage*. Suggest an informal chat about tangential or controversial issues after the regular study is dismissed.

4/ Receive all contributions warmly. Never bluntly reject what anyone says, even if you think the answer is incorrect. Instead ask in a friendly manner, "Where did you find that?" or "Is that actually what it says?" or "What do some of the rest of you think?" Allow the group to handle problems together.

5/ Be sure you don't talk too much as the leader. Redirect

those questions which are asked you. A discussion should move in the form of an asterisk, back and forth between members, not in the form of a fan, with the discussion always coming back to the leader. The leader is to act as moderator. As members of a group get to know each other better, the discussion will move more freely, progressing from the fan to the asterisk pattern.

6/ Don't be afraid of pauses or long silences. People need time to think about the questions and the passage. Never, *never* answer your own question — either use an alternate question or move on to another area for discussion.

7/ Watch hesitant members for an indication by facial expression or body posture that they have something to say, and then give them an encouraging nod or speak their names.

8/ Discourage too talkative members from monopolizing the discussion by specifically directing questions to others. If necessary speak privately to the over-talkative one about the need for discussion rather than lecture in the group, and enlist his aid in encouraging all to participate.

Introduction to 1 Peter

The long hot summer of A.D. 64 was made even hotter on July 19th when Rome was put to the torch. Nero's desire to build demanded a place to build, thus first-century urban renewal, Nero style. The reaction of the populace to this suspected action of the emperor made it imperative that he find plausible culprits. The Christians, already victims of minor persecutions for their faith, bore the brunt of the storm of persecution which followed the fire.

The apostle Peter has been generally acknowledged as the author of this letter, though its excellent literary style and use of the Greek language may well be due to the participation of Silvanus (Silas), identified in 1 Peter 5:12 as the scribe. It was written from a place termed "Babylon" (5:13), very likely Rome, the wealthy, luxury-loving, licentious capital of the Empire.

Peter's letter may have been written late A.D. 63 and received early 64, preceding the outbreak of official Roman persecution against Christians. It was addressed to Christians scattered in the various territories of Asia Minor, many of them converted from paganism, some from Jewish background. Peter's purpose in writing was to strengthen them to face whatever pressures of persecution would come, whether from the malice of those whose sins they no longer shared or the official banning of the Christian faith by Rome.

Discussion 1

Survey of the First Letter of Peter; 1 Peter 1

Read the entire letter through by the following divisions, asking a different person to take each section so that the change in voice will coincide with the change in thought: 1:1-12; 1:13-25; 2:1-10; 2:11-25; 3:1-12; 3:13-22; 4:1-11; 4:12-19; 5:1-14.

The reading should be done in a contemporary translation. Those who are not reading should listen, rather than trying to follow along in their Bibles. If necessary, the same translation can be passed along from reader to reader. Listeners should try to grasp the major themes or ideas of the letter. Some may find it helpful to write brief notes as they listen. Then take five minutes for members of the group to share the ideas and themes they have noted, before beginning the discussion of the first chapter.

1 Peter 1   HOW TO HANDLE TROUBLE

1 Peter 1:1, 2

1. From verses 1, 2 how does the author of this letter describe himself? the people to whom he writes? Describe how each thing Peter says about these people in verse 2 answers a need they are likely to have as a result of their situation in verse 1. What identity, destiny, loyalty, and meaning in life can they find?

2. Compare with Peter's introduction of himself and his readers the various ways in which you might introduce your-

self to others. With what organizations, peoples, places, power-structures today do men and women identify themselves in order to find security and meaning in life?

3. What is revealed about the Trinity of God in verse 2? What is the destiny of the Christian (verse 2)?

4. Share any feelings you, or those you know, have had when, because of company transfers, you have become "exiles" from the part of the country you count as home. Where or how can people find grace and peace in such a situation? How can you help your children in this?

What differences does it make in a person's life whether he considers himself rejected or chosen? How does the question "by whom" one is rejected or chosen affect the situation?

1 Peter 1:3-9

5. What cause do these exiles have for praise and thanksgiving? How were these great benefits obtained? How does Peter describe the durability of their spiritual inheritance? Why is their inheritance safe?

6. If you were to outline from verses 3-5 what the Bible teaches about salvation, what would you include?

7. What perspective and understanding are Peter's readers to have concerning their present troubles? How is the Lord using trouble for good? How can we keep a Christian perspective on our own troubles?

8. What mention of things past, present, and future is made in verses 3-9? How can an understanding of these help us? What various trials and testings do Christians today suffer?

9. If you knew only verses 1-9, what would you know about Jesus Christ? What relationship to him is possible? What is the consequence of this relationship?

1 Peter 1:10-12

10. How do these verses explain the importance of this salvation as it was spoken of in the Old Testament? How did the Old Testament predictions come to be written? What was predicted?

11. What is the good news and how did Peter's readers hear it? How did you hear it? What indicates that these things have cosmic consequences?

12. Why, do you think, does Peter include this parenthetical section (verses 10-12) in his letter? How does it influence your own attitude toward the Old Testament?

[It is suggested that you divide the discussion into two sessions at this point.]

1 Peter 1:13-21

13. In the light of this salvation, what attitudes and actions are appropriate (verses 13-17)? List the verbs in this section, then put the exhortations and commands in your own words.

14. "Holy" means *different* or *separate from* ordinary things and common use and *dedication* to sacred use. "Holiness" is a term for the moral excellence and moral perfection of God.

Considering this, what does it mean for you to be "holy"? Give specific illustrations.

15. What basic reason is given for the Christian to be holy? What added impetus toward holiness is suggested by verses 17-19?

16. What was the price of salvation? Why is it appropriate to remind these Christians of the cost of their salvation immediately after the call to live a holy life? How would you measure your own appreciation of salvation?

17. Why is Christ likened to a lamb? See also Isaiah 53: 7-9; John 1:29; 1 Corinthians 5:7, and 1 Peter 1:2, 11. When was Christ's sacrifice decided upon?

18. In what or whom are your faith and hope put? How would you prove this, if you were called upon to do so?

1 Peter 1:22-25

19. What are the important emphases in this paragraph? How are physical and spiritual birth contrasted? How is spiritual life obtained? What is to characterize the interpersonal relationships of Christian believers?

20. What do these verses reveal about the Word of God? What practical difference should this make in your life?

SUMMARY

1. List from this chapter the things that are *temporary* and the things that are *lasting*.
2. Trace the element of *hope* in this chapter. What reasons for hope would a Christian have, whether in Peter's time or today? How can we share this hope with the younger generation? (What commands does Peter give which will produce an attitude of hope in those who practice them?)
3. Summarize what this chapter teaches about Christ's death and resurrection.
4. According to this first chapter of Peter's letter, what is the gospel?
5. What thoughts in this chapter would you want to convey to Christians today who live where there is danger of prison or death because of their faith?

SO WHAT?

In many parts of the world life is difficult for the true Christian and is likely to become more difficult, but a Christian can choose to live in the perspective of God's activity in history through Jesus Christ. Hope can be a cloak against the temporary winds of trial. The one whose faith is in the risen Lord can set his face into the storm and rejoice with a "great and glorious joy" (verse 8).

Discussion 2 / 1 Peter 2

How to Grow Up

1 Peter 2:1-8

1. Addressing those who have been born anew through the Word of God, against what specific sins does Peter warn his readers? Define each. Why would these people be more susceptible to such sins rather than to sins like murder, adultery, theft?

2. What sins do you think Peter would list as prevalent in most Christian homes today? Why? Why do pressures like those indicated in 1 Peter 1:1, 6, 7 tend to produce such personally destructive attitudes?

3. In verse 2 what alternative attitude, motive, and action are urged? Reflect on how babies are incapable of the sins mentioned in verse 1.

4. How can you best obtain spiritual nourishment? What evidence is there in your life that this is what you really want?

5. What new picture is used to describe Jesus Christ? those who believe in him? What do you understand from verse 5 about who you are, to whom you are related, what your job is, and how you go about it? For *sacrifices* (verse 5), see also Romans 12:1; Hebrews 13:15, 16.

6. From the Old Testament quotations in verses 6-8, how is Jesus viewed by God, by unbelievers, by believers? What is the result of faith in Christ for the believer (verse 6)? the result of rejecting Christ for the unbeliever (verse 8)?

What evidence do you see today of these two opposite views of Jesus and their results? Is Jesus for you the cornerstone upon whom you build your faith, or has he become an obstacle in your path over whom you stumble?

7. What contrast is introduced by *but* in verse 9? List the special things about these believers suggested by each of the four descriptions given in verse 9. Keep in mind the characteristics peculiar to a race, a priesthood, a nation, a people.

8. What responsibility do these Christians have? What changes has God produced in their position? Why would Peter remind them of their past?

9. What does it mean to you personally that you have received God's mercy? How is receiving God's mercy different from receiving his approval?

10. Review the verbs in verses 1-10 which describe what Christians are to be and to do. How can we share this high calling of the people of God?

1 Peter 2:11-17

11. As members of a holy nation, God's own people, this world is a foreign country, a temporary residence for Christians whom Peter calls "aliens and exiles (strangers and refugees) in this world." In view of their status just described, what conduct does Peter urge upon his readers? List the commands, both negative and positive, which he gives.

12. Why are Christians not to retreat from the ungodly society in which they find themselves (verse 12)?

Note — *The day of visitation* may mean the day when God will appear to deliver his people from their persecutors and to judge their oppressors, or it may refer to the time of opportunity to believe in him while he is still visiting his people.

13. Analyze verses 13-17 in terms of a Christian view of freedom. What is freedom's proper use (verse 16)? How may it be used improperly? Is a Christian to be free or to be a slave? Explain. What is God's plan for Christians in society?

14. What is the opposite of each action Peter commands in verse 17? Describe in specific situations how you think a Christian should act in each relationship mentioned. What does it mean to *fear* God?

15. List situations in which you might be considered to be in the position of a servant. (For example — in a job, on a committee of which you are not the chairman, in volunteer services when you are under authority or supervision.)

16. What actions and attitudes are servants to have? toward whom? Why is it appropriate for the Christian to respond like this no matter what the boss is like? Whose approval counts most with you? What are you willing to do to receive it?

17. What experiences should the Christian expect? Why?

18. Outline the example we are to follow as described in verses 21-23. What are the things which Christ did *not* do? What *did* he do? How can really trusting God and his justice help us in situations where we ourselves experience injustice?

19. What did Christ's death do for us (verses 24, 25)? What practical difference ought this to make in our lives?

20. Compare verse 25 with verses 9b, 10; also 1:18, 19. What does each picture add to your understanding of the great salvation that is ours in Jesus Christ?

SUMMARY

1. From this chapter describe the drastic change in position that has occurred in the life of the Christian because of what God has done for him in Jesus Christ.

2. What attitudes should characterize the life of a Christian? What do you feel is the most significant characteristic of the Christian way of life described in this chapter? Why?

3. Peter is writing to people who might easily feel life no longer holds hope or meaning for them. How does this chapter meet their need? any needs you may have?

SO WHAT?

If you are looking for an "Oh, poor you!" message, this chapter is not for you. If we truly understand who we are as possessors of salvation through Jesus Christ, we should stand "nine feet tall" despite outward circumstances. What is more, the moral standard of living to which we are called is the highest. No letting down, no excuses! We are called to be like Jesus Christ in every situation.

Discussion 3 / 1 Peter 3

How to Get Along with One Another

1 Peter 3:1-6

1. What attitudes from the previous section of the letter (2:11-25) do you think are referred to in the expression *likewise?*

2. What special responsibilities do wives have beyond those just mentioned which apply to every Christian? Why doesn't the husband's spiritual state determine the wife's responsibility?

3. What kind of behavior do you think would "speak" (verse 1) to husbands today?

4. What principle concerning dress is suggested in verses 3, 4? How would you analyze your spiritual wardrobe? How does the expression *in God's sight* help us to evaluate the importance of this teaching? While attractive clothes are not forbidden, what are they *not* to be?

5. Apparently Sarah (Genesis 12:11) was a physically beautiful woman, so it is interesting that she is used as an example of the nature of true adornment. What motivated Sarah and the other women mentioned in verses 5, 6?

6. What does it mean in a marriage for the wife to be submissive? What is the alternative? What are the probable results of each of these possibilities? Compare with Colossians 3:18, 19; Ephesians 5:22, 24.

1 Peter 3:7

7. In addition to the attitudes commended in 2:11-25, what is a husband responsible to do?

8. How can a man go about trying to understand his wife?

What things does he need to take into account? In what ways are husband and wife not equal? In what ways are they equal? How should realizing this influence their life together?

9. How practically can a man give his wife honor or status? Why would failure to obey these commands hinder prayer? How does the atmosphere between husband and wife affect the spiritual life of each?

1 Peter 3:8-12

10. Review the progression in Peter's thinking (see 2:18; 3:1, 7, 8). What qualities should characterize the fellowship between Christians (verses 8, 9)? Why? Give an example of a tender heart, a humble mind. How would you define the opposites? How do these things affect interpersonal relationships?

How do these exhortations demand even more from the Christian than those in 2:18-20?

11. In verses 10, 11, Peter quotes from Psalm 34 to confirm his advice to these Christians. What warnings are given and what positive actions are urged in order to live the good life? Compare verse 10 with verse 9 and 1 Peter 2:1. Why, do you think, is there this strong emphasis in this letter?

12. What blessing comes to those who obey verses 8-11? What does the picture in verse 12 reveal? How can Christians do what is right today?

1 Peter 3:13-22

13. What are the various alternatives stated in verses 13-17? How can we overcome fear and anxiety?

14. What quality is to be so evident in a Christian's life that it will cause others to question him about it (verse 15)? See also 1:3.

List the characteristics of the Christian as outlined in verses 15 and 16. What balance is struck between the *word* of witness and the *life* of witness? Why are both essential? Give specific illustrations of an effective witness for Christ in life and word today?

15. Note, as in the previous chapter, that Peter follows his

urgent advice to Christians in verses 13-17 with the encouragement of Christ's example in verse 18. Compare verse 17 with 2:19-21. While a Christian should so live that he will not suffer for evil doing, he may have to suffer because of doing right. What was Christ's own experience in this regard (verse 18)? Why did he die?

16. List all that you learn about Jesus Christ in verses 17-22. What is added here to the picture of Christ given in 2:21-24?

Note — Verses 19, 20 are a parenthesis with difficult and complicated interpretations. Two of the most common are: 1) Between his death and resurrection Christ in his human spirit went to preach to certain spirits in prison in the world of the dead. 2) Christ in the Holy Spirit preached through Noah to the people before the flood.

17. What is the point of the comparison between Noah's experience in the ark and baptism? How is the picture of deliverance completed by Christ's resurrection?

18. What does verse 22 indicate about Christ's present position and power? As Christ's suffering and death were the gateway to his resurrection and glory, what encouragement does this bring to the Christian under persecution by earthly powers? No matter what, who is in control?

SUMMARY

1. Describe the married couple who please the Lord by their attitudes and actions. Give practical suggestions to help couples develop this consideration for each other. Can you trust God to honor your obedience to him in these matters?

2. How can Christians become obedient to the command to have unity of spirit? What do you find draws you to other Christians most meaningfully?

SO WHAT?

Too few of us experience the great potential of the Christian life because we fail to obey its principles in our everyday relationships with one another. We fear other people and fail to reverence Christ in our hearts as Lord! When did you last suffer for righteousness' sake?

Discussion 4 / 1 Peter 4

How to Endure Suffering

1 Peter 4:1-6

1. This section continues the thought of 3:13-18. In addition to obeying the commands in 3:15, 16, how is a believer to arm himself for the conflicts of the Christian life (4:1, 2)? What new motive is to control the Christian?

2. From verses 3, 4, what view do you get of the day in which Peter lived? What formerly characterized the lives of at least some of the Christian believers to whom Peter wrote? How do these sins differ from those against which he earlier warned them in 2:1?

3. How would an awareness of the truth in verse 5 help these Christians to endure abuse and insults from their old associates? To whom are you responsible for the way you live? How can realizing the fact that God is the judge of all help you to withstand ridicule?

4. According to verse 6, why is the gospel preached?

Note — Commentators differ as to whether *the dead* in verse 6 were alive or dead at the time of hearing the gospel. Taking either interpretation, the main thrust of this verse remains the same.

1 Peter 4:7-11

5. List the commands Peter gives in the light of the end of all things. In your own words, what relationships, attitudes, and actions are now important?

6. How do verses 10, 11 emphasize the fact that God is the

source of all we have and all we need? How are we to use what God gives us, what he enables us to do? See also 2 Corinthians 3:5, 6; Romans 12:4-8; John 14:10.

7. How is God glorified? How do we allow his dominion to have expression in our lives?

8. Why, do you think, did Peter say *Amen* at the end of verse 11? How do you feel when Jesus Christ is honored and obeyed? When and how have you seen this happening?

1 Peter 4:12-19

9. Compare verse 12 with 1:6, 7. What purpose is involved? What may the reference to *fire* in both cases suggest?

10. What new element is mentioned as far as the prospect of suffering is concerned? See verses 14, 16.

11. What causes for joy are mentioned in verses 13, 14, 16? How may it be possible for someone today to experience this kind of joy and blessing? Why do you think we do not see more of this suffering and joy?

12. What warnings are included in verses 15, 17, 18? Put them into your own words.

Note — The difficult times already coming upon the Church when Peter wrote were a beginning of the testing and sifting process. If judgment is so severe for the household (people) of God, that facing the unbeliever is indescribable.

13. What ultimate place of safety does the Christian have which the unbeliever does not (verse 19)?

14. What does the expression *suffer as a Christian* or suffer for being a Christian (verse 16) mean to you? Comment on the question: If being a Christian were against the law, would there be enough evidence to convict you?

15. Why is neglecting the gospel of God, failing to obey it, so dangerous (verse 17)? Explain in three or four sentences what this gospel is.

16. How does verse 19 summarize the teaching in this chapter about suffering? How do we learn to trust God? How can we experience his faithfulness? Compare how Jesus trusted God and experienced his faithfulness in 2:21-23; 3:18, 21b, 22.

SUMMARY

1. What grounds for comfort and courage does Peter give to Christians facing the prospect of severer trials than they have yet experienced?

2. The Christian is encouraged to meet his responsibilities to God, to the community of Christians, and to the world. On the basis of this chapter how would you define these responsibilities in contemporary and practical terms?

3. List four specific things you might do to fulfill the responsibilities discussed in the previous question.

SO WHAT?

The twentieth century may go down in history as the age of advertising. Presenting an attractive prospect and promising more than can be delivered has become a way of life. Some even present Christianity with the same adjectives as a travel folder for a Caribbean cruise. This chapter makes no such claims! Peter tells us to look at the experience of our Lord Jesus Christ. He reminds us that as Christians we are to follow him in his sufferings as well as his glory. Although others may be surprised by our new way of life (verses 2, 4), we are not to be surprised if our experience is patterned after the Lord's (verse 12). False advertising leads to disappointment and disillusionment. Those who trust in Jesus Christ will not be disappointed — even in suffering we are assured of his faithfulness.

Discussion 5 / 1 Peter 5
How to Keep Perspective

1 Peter 5:1-5

1. What qualifications does Peter have to exhort the elders? What happens today when those who should exercise authority don't, those who shouldn't do, and no one accepts the authority of others? How can we help to change this situation?

2. What word pictures does Peter use to portray the position and responsibility of elders (verses 2-4)? What experience in his own past would cause Peter to use this term of shepherd? See John 21:15-17.

3. Against what three wrong ways of exerting leadership does Peter warn Christian elders? Describe the positive qualities that are to characterize them. How does the future event referred to in verses 1 and 4 put the work of elders into proper perspective?

Note — The *crown* (verse 4) is compared to the wreath or garland awarded for victory in the Greek athletic festivals (1 Corinthians 9:25). How does this crown differ from those given in athletic games?

4. What difference would it make in your attitude toward those exercising spiritual authority whether they obey Peter's commands in verses 2, 3? What attitude does Peter commend for the younger Christian toward the Christian elders?

5. What attitudes are appropriate between Christians? How can you clothe yourself with humility? What help can you expect from the Lord, both negative and positive (verse 5)?

1 Peter 5:6-11

6. Put into your own words each direct command in verses

29

2-9. How are Christians to act toward one another, toward God, toward the devil?

7. In verses 7-9, list the three statements given as reasons for the actions commanded. Using these three statements as an outline, what points would you include in a talk on "The Christian's Life Pattern"?

8. With verse 7 compare Psalm 55:22. How is casting your cares (anxieties, worries) upon God a part of humbling yourself under his hand (verses 6, 7)? For God's concern for us, see Jesus' words in Luke 12:22-31; Romans 8:32.

Note — "The mighty hand of God" is a figure of speech used in the Old Testament to describe God's intervention in human affairs (Exodus 3:19, 20; 7:5; Deuteronomy 4:34).

9. How does the description of the Christian's adversary in verse 8 fit into the picture of Christians as the flock of God under his shepherd care? What does this portrayal of the devil help you to understand about how to resist him? With verses 8, 9, compare Ephesians 6:10-18, especially verse 16. What action is the Christian to take to withstand the devil?

10. Do you think it is easier to humble yourself before God or before others? Why? Describe a specific experience of responding with humility toward another human being; toward God.

11. What should be the effect of the contrast between the duration of suffering and the duration of glory (verse 10)? Compare with Jesus' words in John 16:21, 22.

12. What precedes the fulfillment of the promise in verse 10? What do the three things promised have in common? How does verse 11 assure the fulfillment of this promise?

1 Peter 5:12-14

13. Who is involved with Peter in sending this letter?

Note — *Silvanus* is generally believed to be Silas, who accompanied Paul on his second missionary journey. (See Acts 18:1, 5; 2 Corinthians 1:19.)

14. How is the purpose of the letter summarized in these final verses?

SUMMARY

1. Why, do you think, did Peter put so much emphasis on the necessity for humility between Christians? What are the results when Christians fail in this?

2. Even in the most difficult circumstances how are we supposed to react toward God? toward one another? toward the devil?

3. What difference do God's present care and his promise of future glory make in how a Christian views any trials and sufferings he endures now for the sake of Christ?

SO WHAT?

One sign of growing up is the ability to tell time. A child struggles to learn to read the face of the clock, but the real sign of maturing is perspective. An infant can't wait five minutes when he is hungry but the mature person understands that "dinner in five minutes" is a very short time to wait. Peter speaks in this chapter of the difference between a little while of suffering and the eternal forever and ever of glory and God's dominion. Let us grow up in our perspective as Christians.

Discussion 6

Review of 1 Peter

1. Note the key words and/or ideas repeated throughout the letter.

2. What seems to you to be Peter's reason for writing this letter?

3. Outline briefly the teaching of this letter about:
   a) salvation
   b) the Christian life
      what is to be sought after
      what is to be avoided
   c) suffering
   d) glory
   e) eschatology (the end times, last things)

4. List the metaphors and similes (word-pictures) which appear in this letter, and what Peter used them to illustrate.

5. What difference would it make to you if you received this letter in circumstances similar to those suggested in it? What specific things would you find most helpful? Why?

6. Fill in the chart on 1 Peter on page 35. Prepare to share the information on your chart with other members of the discussion group.

STUDY NOTES

1 PETER

| 1:1 | 12 | 13 | 25 | 2:1 | 10 | 11 | 25 | 3:1 | 12 | 13 | 22 | 4:1 | 11 | 12 | 19 | 5:1 | 14 |

Title each section and list above.

Describe the major themes of the letter:

List Old Testament references:

List major teachings about Jesus Christ:

Your favorite verse of this letter:

Your personal response to the letter:

2 PETER

| 1:1 | 11 | 12 | 21 | 2:1 | 10a | 10b | 22 | 3:1 | 7 | 8 | 13 | 14 | 18 |

Title each section and list above.

Describe the major themes of the letter:

List Old Testament references:

Evidences for the Trinity of God:

Your favorite verse of this letter:

Your personal response to the letter:

Introduction to 2 Peter

Whether the apostle Peter was the author of this letter has been the subject of discussion for centuries, and the letter was not put into the official list of New Testament documents until the Council of Carthage in A.D. 397, the last book to be included.

Nevertheless, evidence within the letter itself points to Peter as its author: (1:1) the writer's direct claim; (1:14) he expects to die soon, a death predicted by his Lord (compare John 13:36; 21:18, 19); (1:16-18) he saw Christ on the mount of transfiguration. Words and phrases rarely found in other writings are common to both 1 and 2 Peter, and words used in 2 Peter are used almost exclusively by Peter in the book of Acts. If sent by Peter, the letter would have been written about A.D. 66 or 67, shortly before his death.

Whether written by Peter or a teacher of the early church in Peter's name (a literary practice acceptable at that time), the letter of 2 Peter was written to warn the church against false teachers and to encourage Christians to live holy lives in light of Christ's sure return and the consequent coming judgment of this earth with all its works.

Discussion 7

Survey of the Second Letter of Peter; 2 Peter 1

Read the entire letter aloud by the following divisions, assigning a different reader to each section: 1:1-11; 1:12-21; 2:1-10a; 2:10b-22; 3:1-7; 3:8-18.

As the letter is read aloud, ask those listening to jot down the major ideas of the letter. The writer uses many colorful pictorial phrases. What atmosphere is produced by these descriptive terms? Share briefly the answers to these questions before proceeding to the detailed study of chapter 1.

2 Peter 1 HOW TO GROW UP SPIRITUALLY

2 Peter 1:1, 2

1. What indicates that from the beginning this letter was intended to have a wide distribution among Christians?

2. Read verse 1 in several translations. What does it mean to have *a faith of equal standing* with the author of this letter? How does the writer identify himself? According to verse 1, how is such a standing possible? What difference should it make in fellowship with other Christians to realize that our righteousness is not our own?

3. Define *grace* and *peace*. How may we have more and more grace and peace? What is the difference between knowledge *about* and knowledge *of?* How do you get to know a person better? How would these principles apply in getting to know God better?

4. In the phrase *our God and Savior Jesus Christ* (verse 1), what is stated about Jesus Christ?

5. Take five minutes for everyone either to write a paraphrase (put into his own words) or to outline the major points in verses 3, 4. Share your paraphrases and outlines.

6. As Christians what is available to us? What is our calling, our destiny? How can we become like Jesus our Lord?

7. What two things will God's promises enable us to do? Since his promises, his words, are so vital to us, how can we come to know them better? See John 15:5-7. What plan for daily personal encounter with these promises would you suggest?

2 Peter 1:5-11

8. Because of what is potentially theirs, as described in verses 3, 4, what does Peter call upon his readers to do in verses 5-7? Read verses 5-7 in several translations.

9. Write in a column the list in verses 5-7. Note that the first three qualities affect the spirit, the body, and the mind. If you follow these first three commands what changes will there be in you?

10. Trace the development in the last five words in the series of commands. How are you to react to self, to circumstances, to God, to fellow Christians and to all? Review these eight commands and discuss what you feel to be the areas of your greatest personal need.

11. What promise is added and what warning implied (verses 8, 9)? Why is failing to see and to remember (verse 9) so serious? See also Hebrews 2:1; Deuteronomy 32:18, 19. How can you keep from forgetting?

12. What has God already done for the Christian (verses 3, 9b)? Compare with 1 Peter 1:2; 2:9, 21. What is the appropriate response on your part (verses 5, 10)?

13. How would you use this paragraph to refute the accusation that Christianity is a crutch? What kind of life is the Christian expected to live?

14. What promise is given in verse 11 to those who meet

the conditions in verses 5-10? With whose kingdom is this section concerned? Contrast his kingdom with the kingdoms in this world which people serve.

2 Peter 1:12-15

15. How does Peter emphasize the importance of what he has said thus far in this letter? What does he know about his readers? about himself? What is Peter's concern, his purpose for writing? Find the three references to *remembering* in this paragraph.

16. If you have been a Christian for a long time, of what may you need to be reminded? What *truth* do you have (verse 12)?

2 Peter 1:16-21

17. How does Peter prove that his readers had not been told a bunch of fairytales? What was his personal experience? What did he see and hear? See Mark 9:2-8. How did this affect his appreciation of the Old Testament prophecies?

To what does Peter compare the Old Testament (verse 19)? Why is it important? When is a lamp no longer necessary?

18. What is the difference between myths (fables) and Scripture? How did Scripture come to be written? What does this indicate about the importance of Scripture, and about how it must be interpreted? See also 2 Timothy 3:15-17.

SUMMARY

1. In Matthew 16:19 Peter is given the keys of the kingdom. In his letter Peter has outlined how we may gain entrance to the eternal kingdom. Could these be the keys which he shares with us? Summarize God's provisions for us and the efforts we must make to enter the eternal kingdom of Jesus Christ.

2. From the beginning of this letter, Peter expresses a concern that Christians have knowledge. What avenues to this knowledge are developed in chapter 1?

SO WHAT?

God has provided spiritual life for us in Jesus Christ, enabling us to escape the world's corruption and to partake of God's nature. But we must exercise faith to accept God's great promises of power over sin, increasing personal knowledge of Christ, and fruitful excellence of life.

We must make every effort to cooperate with the grace of God, and enter into the paradoxical experience Paul describes when he commands Christians to "work out your own salvation with fear and trembling; for God is at work in you, both to will and to work for his good pleasure" (Philippians 2:12, 13).

Discussion 8 / 2 Peter 2

How to Detect False Teachers

2 Peter 2:1-3

1. In contrast to eyewitness accounts of Jesus' majesty and the Holy Spirit-inspired prophecies of the Old Testament mentioned in chapter 1, against what does Peter warn his readers in this section? To what lengths will these false teachers go? What will be the result for them (verses 1, 3)?

2. What further tragic results are foretold in verse 2? What seem to be the motives of these false teachers (verses 2, 3)?

3. What danger are these people to others? to themselves? Why?

2 Peter 2:4-10a

4. How do verses 4-6 substantiate what is predicted in verse 3b? What three judgments are recalled? How important were the three groups judged?

5. What do you learn about God from these events? Upon what does God put value? What terms are used to describe Noah and Lot? What attitude did Lot have toward the world about him? Why? What verbs tell what the Lord did for Noah and for Lot?

6. What does God's action on behalf of Noah and Lot prove, according to verse 9? What comfort and what warning here are applicable for today?

7. Compare the end of verse 9 with 1 Peter 4:7. What effect should understanding these things have upon your attitudes and actions?

8. How are the sins of verse 10a an insult to God?

9. After the parenthetical statements in verses 4-10a Peter returns to his description of false teachers begun in verses 1-3. What characteristics of these false teachers are emphasized in verses 10b-16?

10. With whom are these false teachers contrasted and compared? What do these comparisons reveal?

11. Why are false teachers appearing within the church so harshly criticized and to be punished so severely? What is the point of the reference to Balaam? (For the detailed Old Testament account of Balaam, see Numbers 22 through 24, but it is not necessary to do so to grasp Peter's reason for referring to him in verse 15.)

12. What outward sins give further proof that the doctrines of these heretical teachers are destructive? What kind of life is the true Christian teacher or leader to live (see 1:4-7)?

13. How can the ordinary Christian avoid being led astray by intellectual and physical enticements? See 1:8, 10, 19-21.

2 Peter 2:17-22

14. Put into your own words the two metaphors used to describe false teachers (verse 17). What does each picture reveal about these false teachers?

15. In verses 18, 19 what helps are given for recognizing a false teacher? What elements would perhaps be included in the message of a false teacher? What contradiction would there be in his life? Compare verse 19 with John 8:34. What is freedom? See John 8:36; Colossians 1:13, 14; 1 Peter 2:16.

16. What tragic regression is described in verses 20-22? What is *worse?* What *would have been better?* Why?

17. In verse 12 these teachers are referred to as irrational animals. How does verse 22 add to this?

18. What effect does the moral climate of a person's life have on the spiritual climate? What effect does the spiritual climate of a person's life have on the moral climate? Why? Suggest specific illustrations.

19. What effect can a turning away intellectually from the message of the Bible have on one's moral values? If God's laws are not absolute, what becomes of the basis for judgment in moral values? How much are we as individuals influenced by the society in which we live today?

SUMMARY

1. Discuss the ways you can protect yourselves and others from the temptations presented by the kinds of spiritual leaders against whom Peter is warning?

2. If these false teachers come, as is suggested, from *within* the church (verses 15, 20), what should Christians do if those in positions of leadership begin to fall into the pattern described in this chapter?

SO WHAT?

J. B. Phillips translated 2 Peter 2:1, ". . . they will be men who will subtly introduce dangerous heresies." Look up *heresy* in a good dictionary and consider its meaning. If we construct doctrines to suit ourselves, picking and choosing portions of Scripture while ignoring others; if we overstress one part of truth and in so doing divide ourselves from other Christians, we are involved in heresy. In every century Christians have neglected some doctrine. Usually in the next century it is over-emphasized and some other doctrine is neglected. The mature Christian studies the Bible carefully to keep a balance. The thoughtful minister aims to preach the total message of Scripture, the whole counsel of God.

Discussion 9 / 2 Peter 3

How to Handle Scoffers

2 Peter 3:1-7

1. Having described in graphic terms in chapter 2 the corruption and consequent judgment of false prophets, Peter now turns to his readers. How does his affectionate term *beloved* affect the atmosphere of his letter at this point?

2. What two things does Peter want his readers to remember? What can be concluded from this about the value of studying the Old and New Testaments? Compare Psalm 119: 49-52.

3. About what sort of people does Peter warn Christians in verses 3 and 4? What rationalization do these scoffers use? What are they counting on? What are they denying?

4. Why do some today deny the certainty of Christ's coming (verse 4)? If anyone promises something, what alternatives do you have concerning his promise? What factors should be taken into consideration before coming to a decision about whether that promise will surely be kept?

5. What three events are referred to in verses 5-7? Which events are past? future? What point does Peter make by these references in answer to the scoffers' declaration in verse 4? What expression does he use twice (verses 5, 7) to explain these happenings?

2 Peter 3:8-13

6. Compare verse 8 with verse 5. What are the two facts to be considered? What danger would there be in ignoring either fact? What personal experience have you observed in which God's timing did not coincide with yours?

7. Discover the contrasting elements in verses 9, 10? What reason is given for the Lord's apparent slowness in keeping his promise to return? What opportunity is still available? What does *like a thief* mean? What choice for each person is implied in verses 9, 10? With what consequences? How and when is that choice made?

8. With verse 9 compare Ezekiel 18:23, 32. What do verses 9 and 10 teach about the Lord? What do you learn about the end of this world?

9. List the verbs in verses 10-12 that describe what will happen to the heavens and the earth. How can modern man appreciate the significance of this prophecy better than those who lived in previous centuries?

10. What perspective and values in life should people have who understand this promise? Why are the things most people pursue ultimately useless? How can we pursue holiness and godliness? Consider Jesus' words in Matthew 5:3-12; 6:19-21.

11. Why can we look forward to and long for such a cataclysmic day? See verse 13. What are we really waiting for?

12. Trace the emphasis on his *promise,* verses 4, 9, 13. What is the total impact of this emphasis? Compare 1 Peter 1:25; Mark 13:31. How reliable is the Lord's promise in your estimation? What difference does this make in your life?

2 Peter 3:14-18

13. Think about your goal in life. What are Christians to be waiting for? (See verses 12-14.) What effect should this have on your conduct? Compare with Mark 13:35, 36. Read verse 14 in several translations. What kind of life does Peter command for the Christian?

Some translations use the expression *at peace with him.* What does this reveal about the meaning of peace? For what kinds of peace do people strive today? Why, do you think, with such little success?

14. What is meant by the Lord's patience or forbearance (verse 15)? (See also verse 9.) What great opportunity does this patience afford? How can we more effectively use this opportunity? What can we do to present Jesus Christ to those in

our home, neighborhood, town? Give specific creative suggestions.

15. Discover at least five things in verses 15b, 16 about the writings of Paul. How do these verses answer the argument that Paul's theology was not that of the apostles?

16. Why is twisting or distorting the Scriptures, either Old or New Testament, a dangerous practice? How are those characterized who do this? How can we protect ourselves against such practices?

17. Contrast the two possibilities that are ours in 17b and 18a. Which is passive? Which is active? What should we be doing? How do we grow in the grace of Christ? the knowledge of Christ? Compare 2 Peter 1:3, 5-8.

18. How may one lose stability? What makes for a stable Christian? Outline some things you would suggest to a new Christian as essential to his spiritual life.

19. "To him belong glory and dominion for ever and ever." "To him be the dominion for ever and ever." "To him be the glory both now and to the day of eternity." (1 Peter 4:11; 5:11; 2 Peter 3:18) What theme prevails in these doxologies? How can Christ have dominion and glory in and through us individually?

SUMMARY

1. Why is the second coming of Christ an essential doctrine for the Christian? What is a Christian view of history? What motivates a Christian's way of life?

2. Describe the *facts* a Christian counts on.

SO WHAT?

In a day of mass communication and mass movements the Christian is more than ever subjected to widely varying influences and teachings. We must beware, as Peter warns, of the influence of false teachers within the framework of Christianity. Twisting the Scripture is not a new practice, but it is as dangerous and prevalent as when Peter wrote. We are protected from it by growing both in grace and in knowledge of the Lord Jesus Christ, by studying the whole Scripture and obeying it, so that we can recognize and reject any distortion.

Discussion 10

Review of 2 Peter

1. List briefly in your own words the commands to Christians in this letter.

2. What does 2 Peter teach about the inspiration and interpretation of Scripture?

3. What kind of error does this letter seek to correct? How can a Christian protect himself from it?

4. What is taught about the second coming of Christ? about the end of the world?

5. What does this letter reveal about God's goal for the Christian?

6. Fill in the chart of 2 Peter on page 36. Be ready to share this information with the group.

NOTES

Marshall Pickering is engaged in a programme of making Marilyn Kunz's and Catherine Schell's group Bible Study outlines, which were originally published in the USA, more widely available in the UK. New titles will be added regularly to the list of titles currently available. The authors suggest the following study guide:

RECOMMENDED FOR SMALL GROUP DISCUSSION BIBLE STUDY

New Groups and Outreach Groups
Mark (recommended as first unit of
    study)
Acts
John, Book 1 (Chaters 1−10)
John, Book 2 (Chapters 11−21)
Romans
Four Men of God (Abraham, Joseph,
    Moses, David)
1 and 2 Peter (Letters to People in
    Trouble)
Genesis (Chapters 1−13)

Groups Reaching People from Non-Christian Cultures
Genesis (Chapters 1−13)
Mark
Romans
Four Men of God (Abraham, Joseph,
    Moses, David)
Philippians and Colossians (Letters
    from Prison)
Patterns for Living with God (Twelve
    Old Testament Character Studies)

Church Groups
Genesis (Chapters 1−13)
Matthew, Book 1 (Chapters 1−16)
Matthew, Book 2 (Chapters 17−28)
1 Corinthians (Challenge to Maturity)
2 Corinthians and Galatians (A Call for
    Help and Freedom)
1 and 2 Peter (Letters to People in
    Trouble)
Psalms and Proverbs
Four Men of God (Abraham, Joseph,
    Moses, David)
Celebrate

Mission Concerns Groups
Luke
Acts
Ephesians and Philemon
The Coming of the Lord (1 and 2
 Thessalonians, 2 and 3 John, Jude)
Romans
1 John and James
Amos (Prophet of Life-Style)

Advanced Groups
Courage to Cope
They Met Jesus (Eight Studies of New
 Testament Characters)
Hebrews
Choose Life (Ten Studies of Basic
 Christian Doctrine)
Amos (Prophet of Life-Style)
The Coming of the Lord (1 and 2
 Thessalonians, 2 and 3 John, Jude)
Prophets of Hope (Haggai, Zechariah,
 Malachi)

Adult and older teens
Matthew, Book 1 (Chapters 1–16)
Matthew, Book 2 (Chapters 17–28)
They Met Jesus (Eight Studies of New
 Testament Characters)
Choose Life (Ten Studies of Basic
 Christian Doctrines)
Celebrate
Courage to Cope
Set Free
Patterns for Living with God (Twelve
 Old Testament Character Studies)

Biweekly or Monthly Groups
They Met Jesus (Eight Studies of New
 Testament Characters)
Set Free
Celebrate
Courage to Cope
Psalms and Proverbs

**How to Start a Neighborhood Bible
Study**
(A Guide to Discussion Study) is also
 available.